Cracked Sidewalks and French Pastry

Al McGuire
September 7, 1928–January 26, 2001

Cracked Sidewalks and French Pastry

The Wit and Wisdom of Al McGuire

Tom Kertscher

Foreword by Dean Smith

THE UNIVERSITY OF WISCONSIN PRESS

The University of Wisconsin Press
1930 Monroe Street
Madison, Wisconsin 53711

www.wisc.edu/wisconsinpress/

3 Henrietta Street
London WC2E 8LU, England

1   3   5   4   2

Printed in Canada

Designed by Jane Tenenbaum

Library of Congress Cataloging-in-Publication Data
Kertscher, Tom, 1961–
Cracked sidewalks and French pastry : the wit and wisdome of Al McGuire /
Tom Kertscher ; foreword by Dean Smith.
pp.   cm.
ISBN: 0-299-18310-6 (cloth : alk. paper)
1. McGuire, Al—Quotations. 2. McGuire, Al—Pictorial works.
3. Marquette University—Basketball—History. 4. Basketball coaches—United States.
I. Title.
GV884.M27 K47   2002
796.323/092—dc21   2002005958

To my daughter Hailey,
who showed me how to love

Contents

Foreword

Al McGuire had an unorthodox, candid, clever way of expressing himself, and in the process made many people laugh. He also made them *think*. Closer examination of his words reveals not only a humorist but also a philosopher, social commentator, and man who did not avoid controversial issues.

He was the closest thing the sports world had to a modern-day Will Rogers.

There was a dichotomy at work here. When the bright lights came on, Al enjoyed center stage and performed accordingly. Or, as he used to say, "I like to have the brass ring." On the other hand, the private Al McGuire was an equally interesting personality in his own right, a man who enjoyed long, solitary walks and motorcycle trips to small towns where he loved to browse at antique shops.

Tom Kertscher's book—both words and pictures—helps shed additional light on the complex, complicated, and intelligent man that was Al McGuire. Al and I became friends in 1959. We were young coaches whose common denominator was Frank McGuire. Al was Frank's basketball captain at St. John's; I was Frank's assistant coach at North Carolina.

My North Carolina team used to scrimmage Al's team from Belmont Abbey College, which is located near Charlotte. North Carolina lost to Al's Marquette team in the 1977 NCAA championship game. I recruited his son, Allie. After Al took the head coaching job at Marquette, he and several of his Milwaukee friends would come to North Carolina in the springtime, and I often joined him to play golf. I enjoyed his company immensely. I was honored when he asked me to be the "inductor" for his enshrinement in the Basketball Hall of Fame.

Al was as unpredictable as a prairie wind. While most college coaches spend their careers fighting for a chance to play in the NCAA tournament, Al turned down a bid in 1970 because he was upset the selection committee assigned Marquette to a regional in Lubbock, Texas. Saying he wasn't in the market for any livestock, Al refused to take his team to Lubbock. Instead, Marquette went to New York to play in the NIT—and won it. A little later, feeling that a high school basketball player was getting too much national attention as a prominent recruit, Al called him on the spur of the moment and said: "I want you to know we don't have a scholarship for you at Marquette." It didn't matter to Al that the kid wasn't considering Marquette. He nevertheless wanted to let him know that there was at least one college coach who didn't think the kid had invented basketball. In such matters, Al was about as subtle as a train derailment.

Whether coaching his team, or giving a cocky teenager a shot of reality, Al had exquisite timing. When it came to expressing himself, he had a style that was impossible to emulate. He didn't think as much in words, sentences and paragraphs as he did in pictures. For instance, Al was happy at the beach among family and friends. Thus, happiness was easy to see in his mind's eye: "seashells and balloons."

Al and I shared a long belief, rare at the time, that some of our players *should* leave college early, *if* it was a lock that they could reach financial security by signing an NBA contract. When asked why he urged Jim Chones, his star center, to leave Marquette early to play professional basketball, Al replied: "I looked in my refrigerator and it was full. I looked in Jim's and it was empty. Easy choice."

An outstanding coach and a brilliant amateur psychologist, Al was respected by his players, who did as he asked. He knew how to prepare them, mentally and strategically. He also had a knack for getting into the head of some opposing coaches. Once, when Belmont Abbey played Lefty Driesell's Davidson College team in the old Armory Auditorium in Charlotte, Al left his place on the bench during the close game to sit in the stands with a friend. "Hey, Lefty," Al shouted towards the Davidson bench, "if you need me, I'm up here." A flustered Lefty took a timeout and urged the officials to make Al return to his bench, which they did. Al returned to a standing ovation from the crowd. Without a doubt, he knew how to take over a room.

Of course, when a personality is so colorful, humorous, and quotable, there's a danger his genius could be lost in a sea of funny quotes. I found Al to be as much of a street philosopher as a humorist. When he coached at Marquette, his route from home to work brought him to a fork in the road: a left turn took him to the office, while a right turn took him to the country for a day of reflection, a direction he took at least once a month. That's why he often advised his friends, "Don't forget to take some right turns."

There's a picture in this book that reveals more about my friend Al

McGuire than I ever could. He is shown standing by the bed of a critically ill child. The photo shows compassion and caring, as well as sadness etched in Al's face. Depending on the occasion, he could be as tough as iron or as soft as putty. Al himself would describe such a man as "a man's man," which he certainly was.

More than his many humorous sayings and his hundreds of coaching victories, this single picture captures the essence of Al. Certainly, I'm grateful our paths crossed and a friendship developed. This book will help keep Al's memory alive.

Dean Smith

Preface

Al McGuire possessed an uncommon ability to touch people. He made his most profound effect on me after he had gone.

The idea for *Cracked Sidewalks and French Pastry* came in March 2001, two months after McGuire passed away. I was in Minneapolis attending my first Final Four—the same college basketball championship that Marquette University had won so dramatically in 1977, in McGuire's final game as a coach.

I don't know why the inspiration came to me. But I believe it was partly Al's doing.

○

Like many people in the Milwaukee area in the 1970s, I was a Marquette fan. Taking after my dad, I collected newspaper clippings during the Warriors' championship season and made a scrapbook. I remember putting a picture of star player Butch Lee on the cover.

But after the championship, McGuire retired. I soon finished high school in Cedarburg and left the area. I didn't follow college basketball closely anymore.

Then in 1998 I made a homecoming to Milwaukee, and, for reasons I couldn't quite understand, I felt drawn to Marquette. I bought season tickets and went to the games. But not until that trip to the Final Four, and the idea for *Cracked Sidewalks*, did that nagging feeling go away.

I stopped feeling merely drawn to Marquette and started feeling connected to McGuire.

○

In reading about Al and in talking with people who knew him, I came to feel a deeper appreciation for the preciousness of life. It remained a force inside me throughout my work on the book.

I attribute that feeling to the fact that Al McGuire was a special man, one of God's great gifts. Those of you who knew him appreciate that more than I ever could—though there were times during my work when I believe I felt his presence.

As much of a showman as McGuire was, he probably would not have been behind a book like this; he shrank from such things. Yet, for some reason, Al McGuire touched me in his incomparable way. The result is what you are about to read.

I hope that somewhere in these pages, Al McGuire will touch you, too.

Acknowledgments

I want to thank a few of the many people who helped me with this book:

Matt Blessing at Marquette University, who was exceptionally accommodating in helping me do my research, and Rosemary Jensen, who also made my research easier.

Jack Byrne of Sternig-Byrne Literary Agency, Milwaukee, and Steve Salemson at the University of Wisconsin Press, who helped me navigate the path to getting this book in print.

Greg J. Borowski, my friend and colleague, who was always willing to be a sounding board.

Michael Baron-Jeffrey, my longtime friend, who was willing to help at every turn.

Jim Kertscher, my dad, who taught me to appreciate history and the exceptional people in sports.

And Barbara Kertscher, my mom, who is always close to my heart.

Cracked Sidewalks and French Pastry

Cupcakes and Sand Fights

McGuire on Coaching

1

Al McGuire became a transcendent figure in coaching because of what he did off the court.

During a time of tense race relations in the 1960s and '70s, McGuire was a white coach who pioneered recruiting in the black ghettoes. And more than 90 percent of his players at Marquette earned degrees.

But those successes probably would not be known had McGuire not also been a winner. Besides capturing the national championship in 1977, the Warriors won 295 games and lost 80 (78 percent), appeared in nine NCAA tournaments, and won eighty-one home games in a row during McGuire's thirteen seasons. His twenty-year record as a head coach was 404–144.

McGuire's genius showed during the final moments of a game. When it came to setting plays, substituting players, outthinking the opposing coach, and minding the referees there was no mind keener than McGuire's.

In Marquette's semifinal victory on the way to the national championship, Jerome Whitehead made a dramatic last-second basket after catching a tipped full-court pass from Butch Lee. But the victory wasn't sealed until the chaotic moments after the final buzzer, when McGuire used his fast talk and street smarts to convince the officials that the basket should count.

"He could think bing-bing-bing," Jimmy Breslin, the Pulitzer Prize–winning columnist and a boyhood pal of McGuire's, recalled in a recent interview. "When did he lose a one-point game? Two in his life? Nobody could run a game like that."

A team should be an extension of a coach's personality. My teams are arrogant and obnoxious.

I like SRO. You need charisma. There should be electricity. When I walk into the arena, the first thing I do is look at the four corner seats. If those are sold, I've done my job.

I never saw a ballplayer play in high school that I recruited, and I only recruited blue-plate specials.

○

My rule was I wouldn't recruit a kid if he had grass in front of his house. That's not my world. My world was a cracked sidewalk.

○

We don't say "my man," and we don't slap five. We don't patronize. We shake hands and say, "Mr. Lee, I'm happy to meet you."

Right: McGuire with Paul Carbins and Bob Wolf in 1965.

I've never blown a whistle, looked at
a film, worked at a blackboard, or
organized a practice in my life.

○

I feel the game more than I know it,
that's the way I've always been.
I can talk one thing—winning.
But don't ask me how. My assistant,
Hank Raymonds, was in charge of that.
I never studied the game.

I'm not sure I have the basketball knowledge of a good high school coach. I don't know if I coach. I think I'm more like the master of ceremonies. I create a party on the court and keep it going.

13

I don't discuss basketball.
I dictate basketball.
I'm not interested in philosophy classes.

I'm the boss. The players know it. There's a give and take, but in the end I'm the dictator.

○

People can't understand my players screaming back at me, but it's healthy. Also, I notice that the screaming always comes when we're fifteen, twenty ahead. When it's tied, they're all listening very carefully to what I have to say.

○

My era is over. Dictator coaches are finished. I was good for the "Burn, baby, burn" atmosphere. It's time now for coaches who sit in dens.

I don't believe in looking past anybody.
I wouldn't look past the Little Sisters of
the Poor after they stayed up all night.

You've got to break up cliques or
you'll find players husband-and-wifing-it
out on the court.

We don't run a plantation here. I want and expect my players to get degrees, even if it takes more than four years.

I'm not saying that they were Einsteins;
they were marginal students.
But every ballplayer who ever touched
me has moved up his station in life.
And the players moved up my station.

I see either roses or weeds. It's definitely going to depend upon if the players really love each other or just make believe and have their love affairs with the semi-agents who will tout them and blow their heads out of proportion. . . . It all gets down to love. If we have love, we'll be good. If we don't, we'll be bad.

If a player leaves Marquette and doesn't
have some of my blood in him, then I
don't think I've done a good job.

Coaching is not the ultimate. I never
liked coaching. There's got to be more to
life than hangin' up jock straps.

○

It's a profession in which, the longer you
stay, the closer you are to being fired.

Hank Raymonds and Rick Majerus were McGuire's top assistants at Marquette.

On his assistant coaches:

I just put on the cocktail dress and go to the parties. They're the ones who do the real work.

You've got to remember, it's a game.
If we lose, a new star will appear
in the east.

Keep in mind that winning is only important in major surgery and all-out war, and you'll have a leg up on staying loose and winning ballgames.

If winning weren't important,
nobody would keep score.

McGuire celebrates atop a table after Marquette beat the University of Wisconsin on a last-second shot. Wisconsin coach John Powless is in the foreground at left. In the crowd, the father of UW players Kim and Kerry Hughes responds to McGuire with a hand gesture.

If you have a sincere desire to improve yourself academically; are willing to work harder than ever before; want to be part of a program demanding excellence; want to be No. 1; expect to be treated with personal dignity and respect; will put team play above individual accomplishment; want to learn what life is all about; do not want to be used; want to be accepted as a person, not as a jock; then Marquette University's basketball program is for you.

Well, here we go again, the charisma of the roundball, peaks and valleys, lost families, fathers that are coaches, mothers that are overly possessive, faculty members that feel sports are ruining society, officials that have bad nights, ankles that won't heal, girls that become mothers too soon, rumors of acid and grass, quotes out of context, limited use of gym, no hot water, who stole the socks?

McGuire coached at Belmont Abbey College in North Carolina before coming to Marquette. During one game there, he was so irked about fouls being called on his team that he handed his sports coat to a referee, saying:

Here, take this, you've taken everything else from me tonight.

Complaining during the 1977 NCAA tournament that referees had been "brainwashed" by the NCAA into making calls against him:

It's about time that some people started to realize that I'm not a bum in a bowery, or a wino in a hallway, or a pimp on a corner. I know my profession, I know it well, and I've worked at it hard. All my life I've worked at it hard.

McGuire and Hank Raymonds celebrate in 1965 after Marquette defeated Wisconsin
for the second time that season.

The nicest thing about coaching
is that one day you feel like you can play
handball against a curb, and on other
days you feel like you can
fly to the moon.

Just once I'd like to let something get by me without yelling about it. But in my type of coaching there's no room for happiness.

Look, if you're into coaching heavy, into the blackboard, if you're going to charge up the hill into the machine guns, then you might as well stay at St. Ann's in the fifth grade.

○

The people who know basketball,
their elevators don't go to the top.

McGuire reacts to a typically rough and tumble play during the
1977 national championship game.

A player has to give all he has for you. It has to be a personal thing. He has to feel a win and he has to feel a loss. He has to be willing to give up a dented nose or a tooth or a bent rib. He isn't playing basketball for you if he isn't willing.

○

If you haven't broken your nose in basketball, you haven't really played. You've just tokened it.

○

What it takes to be a great player, beyond raw talent, is self-centeredness and a certain numbness to the crowd. Superintelligent people can't be superb athletes. They're too aware.

On defeating Cincinnati in the Midwest Regional in Omaha on the way to the 1977 NCAA championship:

There is no way they could defense my lucky suit. They tried to steal it, but we got it back. It's not lucky at home, but it is on the road. It's made of traveling threads.

◦

When we lost our third straight game at home and were going on a five-game road series, I had given up. Outside of my lucky suit, I don't know what caused our turnaround. I honestly don't know what happened. Maybe they stopped listening to the coach.

On defeating North Carolina in the finals in Atlanta:

It was magic. The next thing I knew, I was crying where Sherman burned the city down.

○

I'm not afraid to cry. All I can think about is,
Why me? After all the jocks and socks.
All the odors in the locker room. All the fights
in the gyms. Just the wildness of it all.
And to have it end like this . . .

○

You'd rather cry alone. It was a thing pent up
after all the years of my jerking around in
sports. It was probably a million-dollar cry.
I think it changed how I was perceived by
a lot of people throughout the country.
But I was never ashamed of my emotions.

McGuire, Raymonds, and Majerus during the final moments of Marquette's national championship victory.

How winning the championship affected McGuire:

You get compassion. You lose the soot on your face, let your hair grow, put on your beach shoes. . . . You lose your obnoxiousness, your surliness. The game isn't everything because you become more intelligent. You see more.

McGuire celebrates the national championship with Bernard Toone,
who had cut down one of the nets, and Jerome Whitehead.

I've always been the
bridesmaid. More like
a lunch-pail, tin-hat
type of person. I never
thought I'd really win.
I'm a positive thinker,
but I always thought
I'd come in second.

[Coaching] didn't quiver anymore. . . .
If something doesn't quiver,
I have no excitement in it.

○

I had my moment on the stage.
The trick in life is to know when to leave.

○

It's time. Every carnival has an end.
Circuses close. Honeymoons come
to an end sooner or later and Marquette
has provided me with an extended
honeymoon. It's been super,
but now it's time.

Barefoot in the Wet Grass

McGuire on Life

2

Al McGuire thought in pictures, and they made his words vivid.

"Cracked sidewalks" described the slums where McGuire recruited his best basketball players. The fancy moves those players made on the court were "French pastry."

But McGuire is a lasting figure not because of how he spoke—but because he had something to say.

"He worked hard at not being a cliché," said Bill Dwyre, who covered McGuire in Milwaukee and is now the sports editor for the *Los Angeles Times*. "He recognized that other coaches were clichés."

McGuire made nutty, witty, and poignant observations on sports and on life—and he offered a few words to live by, too.

I think the world is run by C students.

If the waitress has dirty ankles, the chili is good.

You know what pressure is? It's when
the cheerleaders are jumping and you
don't notice their breasts.

It's so ridiculous to see a golfer with a one-foot putt and everybody saying "Shhh" and not moving a muscle. Then we allow a nineteen-year-old kid to face a game-deciding free throw with seventeen thousand people yelling.

I think everyone should go to college and get a degree and then spend six months as a bartender and six months as a cab driver. Then they would really be educated.

◉

I don't know why people question the academic training of a student athlete. Half the doctors in the country graduated in the bottom half of their class.

Life is what you allow yourself not to see.

McGuire before the start of the 1981 Al's Run. The annual charity event, begun in 1978, has raised $4.8 million for Children's Hospital of Wisconsin. McGuire launched the run as a way to thank the southeast Wisconsin community for their support.

Sports is a coffee break.

I've never met a young person who wore galoshes whom I thought was successful. In fact, I guarantee you that anyone who wears galoshes to the office never misses a coffee break.

○

When a guy takes off his coat, he's not going to fight. When a guy takes off his wristwatch, watch out!

○

The only mystery in life is why kamikaze pilots wore helmets.

All love affairs end. Eventually the girl is
gonna put curlers in her hair.

○

If you marry a good-looking woman,
she may leave you. Of course, an ugly
woman may leave you too,
but you won't care.

○

Every obnoxious fan has a wife
[at] home who dominates him.

McGuire with his grandson, A. J. McGuire, after the 1980 Al's Run.

Help one kid at a time. He'll maybe go back and help a few more. In a generation, you'll have something.

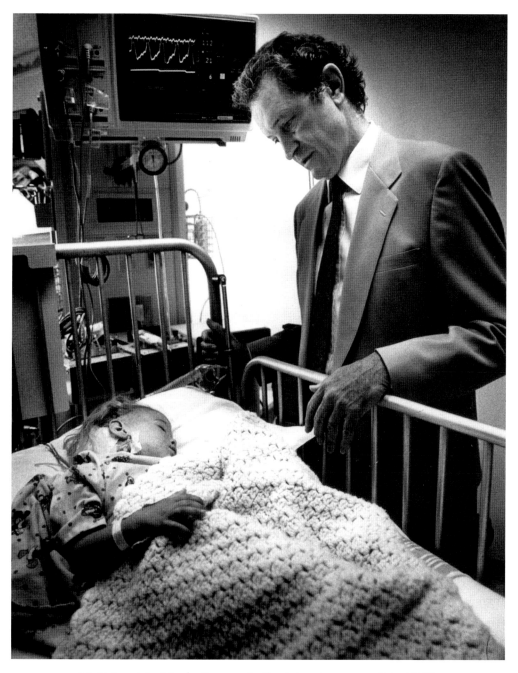

McGuire visits Nicole Bessner in the intensive care unit in 1989.

There's always going to be problems, and I feel the greater the problems for a generation the greater that generation is going to be.

If someone calls you, the third thing he says is usually the reason he called.

Anyone who offers to double your money, walk away. If he offers to make you 20 percent, hear him out.

Never take a towel out of a motel room
—take a TV set.

Never undress until you die.

Dream big. Don't be just another guy going down the street and going nowhere.

We rush for the stars as
we crawl toward our graves.

You're born alone, you die alone.

McGuire's version of "live in the moment":

Congratulate the temporary.

MARQUETTE UNIVERSITY
1965-66 BASKETBALL GUIDE
For Press-Radio-TV

God didn't miss any of us.

McGuire and Katie Pedersen, wearing number one,
before the 1991 Al's Run. Katie, then twelve years old,
had been diagnosed with a brain tumor.

Stalking the sidelines, McGuire was as intense a game coach as there was.
But he often preached to his players, "Use basketball, don't let it use you."

McGuire beat out Hank Raymonds for the head coaching job at Marquette,
but McGuire kept Raymonds on as an assistant. Raymonds kept all the vital details in order,
enabling McGuire to remain the free spirit that he was.

McGuire prided himself on winning, but also on his ability to coach off the court.
"Dealing with problems, with differences—that's coaching.
Running patterns is not coaching."

"I coached by instinct, by feeling. Coach Norm (Sloan) was in love with basketball—still is. I was not. To me, basketball was just a means to an end," McGuire wrote in a foreword to a book by Sloan.

McGuire's son, Al (12), and Raymonds's son, Steve (21), played together at Marquette in the early 1970s.

During their second meeting, McGuire handed Raymonds a blank check and asked him to fill in the amount to pay for the home McGuire was buying in Brookfield. Raymonds said McGuire told him to do whatever he wanted as assistant coach. "Here was a guy I never met, who put his trust in me," Raymonds was quoted as saying years later. "After that blank check, it wasn't a joke anymore."

Right: In one of the most memorable images in college basketball, McGuire showed his emotions as the final buzzer sounded in Marquette's national championship victory over North Carolina in 1977.

McGuire didn't attend all of Marquette's practices.
"My philosophy is that I get tired of my ballplayers and they get tired of me."

McGuire was involved in Al's Run from its launch in 1978 through 1997.
The charity race attracted thousands of runners, including this throng in 1983, to downtown Milwaukee.

McGuire valued his assistants, Hank Raymonds and Rick Majerus,
but he insisted on being in charge. "Only one of us can wear the brassiere."

"A lot of coaching is what you choose to do, not to see," McGuire said.
"That is hypocritical, of course, but it is also true."

McGuire's sister Kathleen, longtime friend Jerry Savio, and McGuire
at McGuire's daughter Noreen's wedding.

McGuire with friends during one of their trips to Las Vegas. Seated, left to right: McGuire, former player Ed Janka and his girlfriend. Standing: McGuire's wife Pat and son Robbie, and Georgene and Jerry Savio.

The national championship team. Seated, left to right: Ulice Payne Jr., Jim Boylan, Butch Lee, Gary Rosenberger and Mark Lavin. Standing: Mark Stack, Mark Paget, assistant coach Hank Raymonds, Bernard Toone, Bo Ellis, Jerome Whitehead, McGuire, Craig Butrym, Robert Byrd, staff members Kevin Byrne and Jeff Bertsch.

Pure Park Avenue

McGuire on McGuire

3

Cocky as a coach and boisterous as a broadcaster, Al McGuire seemed like the life of the party. But out of the spotlight, he often sought down time. Perhaps that's why, even after fortune and fame, he continued to relate to the "two-dollar bettor."

Barbara Roncke, the first woman sports editor at the *Marquette Tribune* student paper, remembers when McGuire ran into her on a Marquette road trip in Kentucky. He wanted to know her plans before the game later that day and was happy to hear she would be sightseeing.

"Good. Give me the key to your room. I want to hide out," Roncke recalled McGuire saying. And that's what he did.

I'm an Einstein of the streets and
an Oxford scholar of common sense.

○

You cannot have a bland feeling about me.
Either I'm a showboating son of a bitch, or
I'm the darling that everyone picks on.

When I'm losing, they call me nuts.
When I'm winning, they call me eccentric.

I was the Houdini who did his disappearing act. I know that 85 percent of me is buffalo chips and the other 15 percent is rare talent. I'd stay in that 15 percent in the mental toughness, the media, keeping an eye on the elephant, not the mice, and extending the life of the extinct kiwi bird, which is nocturnal.

McGuire played at St.
John's University from
1948 to 1951 and in the
NBA from 1951 to 1954.

I stayed in the [NBA] three years
by diving over press tables
and starting fights.

Sometimes I say things I shouldn't.
I go berserk. If I were a university,
I'd never hire me.

I only comb my hair if
there are four people in the room,
and if there are four people,
I'm getting paid.

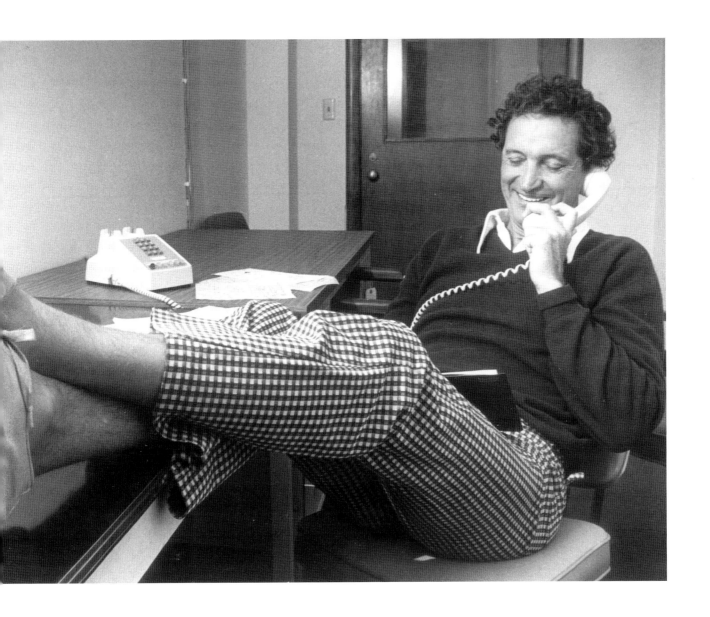

I don't like executive offices. Everyone is usually looking at their watches and burping.

My personal style is not negotiable.
That's how I fly. If you don't like
my onion sandwiches, too bad.
I can't change.

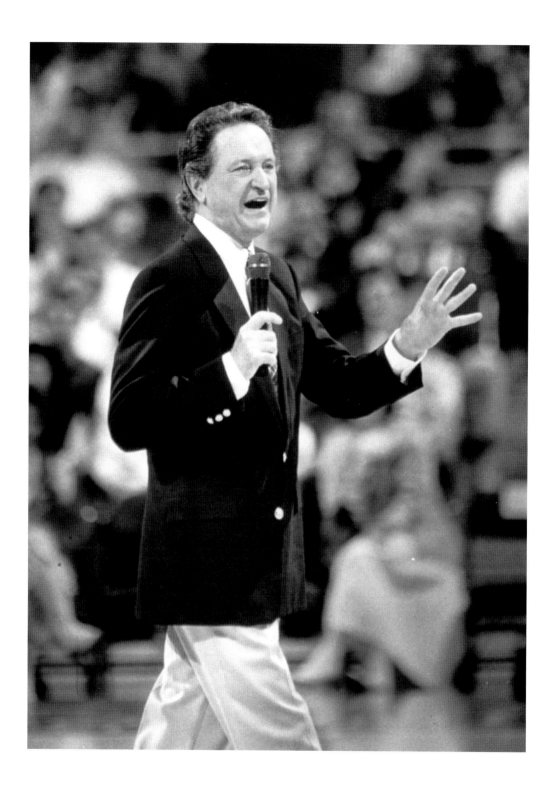

I don't really know what it is
not to be a celebrity. I like to have
smoke rings blown at me.

○

A lot of my stuff is an act. I don't know
when my act ends anymore. What can
I do? It's a way of life.

I want to keep the pulse of the parking-lot attendant—the country club or golf course is not where it's at. The pulse is on the cracked sidewalks. If you lose that, life's not worth living. As a person, I hope I never change.

I honestly don't know when I'm acting and when I'm not. I flirt with it, but not intentionally. It's a gray area, it's a limbo. It's a mucus-type thing that flirts with me and you spin out now and then and go into the minus pool, then sometimes you'll turn around and pyramid up.

I always wanted to sit in the front seats on the bus. I always wanted to be called "Coach." Those were the only two things that were important to me.

Butch Lee and McGuire celebrate after a last-second shot in the semifinal game propelled Marquette into the 1977 national championship game.

I don't know why life has been so good, and that's legit. I don't know why it's been so good to me. I guess mainly it's because of the people I touch.

We had someone from the FBI
talk to us before the season and he told
us there were three places in town
we should declare off-limits.
I had been hanging out in two of them.

I like seashells and balloons, ribbons and medals, bare feet and wet grass.

○

Seashells and balloons is bare feet and wet grass. It means a light breeze. You know, a light breeze that would maybe move a girl's skirt a little. It's sweater weather. A malted, you know, a shake. The gentleness of it. The wholesomeness of it. It's tender. That type of thing.

I don't know where the devil I came up with it.
People, when they hear it, if they are of that
certain type of quality, they understand
what a seashell is and what a balloon is.

I really like who I am. I have a blind side,
Achilles' heels and closet things, like everyone
else. But if I had the run to do all over again . . .
the only thing I would change is
I would have grown up with my children.

I was marvelously lucky to touch and seize a
rising and striving world; a reckless world, filled
with the curiosity of life itself; a vivid and
violent world welcoming every challenge; a
world hating and adoring and fighting and
forgiving; in brief, a world which was a world.

Pictured, from left, at the start of the 1974–75 season:
Butch Lee, Bo Ellis, Earl Tatum, McGuire, Rick Campbell, and Lloyd Walton.

A lot of people give me credit for having a special rapport with blacks, especially when I was coaching. But I was no crusader. It was just that racism never came up with me in my life in basketball, as a player, a coach, or whatever. At the end of the day I'd go where I lived, and they'd go where they lived. But during the day I can honestly say I was never aware of the color of anyone's skin.

I wasn't different.
I was ahead of my time.
I still am.

Calliopes, Clergy, and Raquel Welch

McGuire on Everything Else

4

Al McGuire could make a lasting impression in a matter of minutes.

In 1978, just before giving a speech at a Syracuse University basketball banquet, McGuire stopped to chat with Darwin "Buddy" Houseman, a young man in a wheelchair who had spina bifida.

McGuire had already been announced at the podium and the crowd was waiting, but he remained in the back of the room for several minutes kneeling at Buddy's side in conversation. After McGuire went to the podium, people who had watched the exchange applauded for Buddy in one of his proudest moments before his death less than a year later.

"My guess is he is a man who decided those moments were important," said Buddy's cousin, DeDe Snyder. "It was important for Buddy, but I think it was important for Al, too. I think that's probably how he kept a humble nature and kept in touch with who he really was."

There is a nice feeling at two in
the morning to see a beer sign. It's
somewhere you can place a bet or have
an affair or play a jukebox or whatever.
Of all the places I know on Earth, it
seems to be the most wholesome. You're
not walking into anything that you have
to prep yourself for. When you go in, you
know what's there and what's expected
of you. If you want to join in, you can.
If you want to slip down to the end of
the bar and cry in your beer,
you can do that, too.

I don't go to funerals, because I bought you a drink while you were alive. Anyway, the crowd at a funeral is governed by the weather.

(More than one thousand mourners attended McGuire's funeral on a cold and rainy January night in Milwaukee.)

What do you think you're doing?
We're trying to get a show done out here!

McGuire laughs as Billy Packer makes remarks at a function. McGuire and Packer often
ribbed each other during college basketball broadcasts, but were good friends.
Along with Dick Enberg, they formed one of the sport's best broadcast teams.

When legendary University of Kentucky coach Adolph Rupp
called McGuire "son" during the 1968–69 NCAA tournament,
the young upstart coach shot back:

Don't call me son unless you're going to include me in your will.

On gamblers who befriend college athletes:

You must try to teach your players that if there are creeps hanging around, there's a reason. It's like when you bring flowers home to your wife and say there's no reason. There's a reason.

McGuire (59) chases legendary Penn State football coach Joe Paterno (29) in a 1945 New York City high school Turkey Bowl.

On football players:

They do one-arm push-ups so that they can count with the other hand.

On his disappointment when NBC, which had broadcast the regular-season NCAA basketball games, was outbid by CBS to carry the postseason tournament games:

It's like getting all the dances with the girl, but when it comes time to take her home and get in the rumble seat, it's CBS that is touching the soft spots.

On having microphone trouble during a speech:

I've had more dead mikes than an Irish funeral.

On Texas Tech University coach Bob Knight:

Bob reminds me of Alexander the Great, who conquered the world and then sat down and cried because there was nothing left to conquer.

◎

On former St. John's University coach Lou Carnesecca:

Looie is the quintessential gym rat. But he's also a people rat. He magnets them.

◎

On college presidents:

They still think that anyone who took physical education or spends time in a building that has a sweat odor is a peasant. They think: "We got to put up with guys walking around with no necks." But they can't shake and bake too much because the alumni like it.

On Harold Miner, a University of Southern California player, and his ritual before shooting a free throw:

He goes through so many things at the foul line, I think I'm watching *Macbeth*.

○

On Geoff Crompton, a 300-pound University of North Carolina player, who had recently lost fifteen pounds:

That's like the *Queen Mary* losing a deck chair.

○

On agents who represent players:

I think an agent should be paid by the hour. I don't believe anyone should own a percentage of anyone else. That's one of the reasons we fought the Civil War.

On the Final Four college basketball championships:

It's a calliope, cotton candy, the guy with the hook who wants to see the girls with the big breasts, to show you the power.

○

For those who get to the Final Four, it's like automatically winning a championship. It's getting there that's important. If you get to the Final Four, it brings you to the next strata for recruiting. It puts you in a Technicolor visibility avalanche.

Who the hell can live in Montana?
The first forty-eight hours are beautiful.
But after that, the mountains don't move.

○

I come from New York where,
if you fall down, someone will
pick you up by your wallet.

Describing action in a 1988 Olympics game with players from
the Soviet Union whose names he couldn't remember:

Igor the Terrible passes to the Red Machine!

Marquette player George "Sugar" Frazier once told McGuire
he should be starting ahead of McGuire's son, Allie:

Sugar, Allie is my son, and I love him. For you to
start, you must be better than he is. Right now,
it's a tie. And Allie wins all pushes.

On why he advised Marquette player Jim Chones to leave school early and enter professional basketball with a million-dollar contract:

I looked in my refrigerator and it was full. I looked in Jim's and it was empty. Easy choice.

On Dean Meminger, one of McGuire's first star recruits at Marquette:

Dean Meminger was quicker than
11:15 Mass at a seaside resort.

On Bo Ellis before the 1976–77 national championship season:

If it's our turn to part the sea,
then Bo is our Moses.

To me, even the worst college cheerleader is better than the best pro cheerleader. The pro cheerleaders put on a little too much rouge and seem to have too many places where you can hang your hat. But in college, they just seem to be turned on. It seems to be a legitimate genuine concern. They don't seem to be looking for the red light on the camera.

○

You can always tell the Catholic schools by the length of the cheerleaders' skirts.

McGuire's threat to an arena official before a game at Bradley University in 1965 after Barbara Roncke, the first female sports editor of the Marquette Tribune *student newspaper, wasn't allowed to sit in the press row:*

She doesn't sit in the press row,
we don't play this game.

○

If women aren't interested in a sport,
it will eventually die.

McGuire grew up poor and once described the conditions
of his family life using a football reference:

When we tossed the dog a bone,
he'd call for a fair catch.

○

McGuire's family ran a tavern while he was growing up
in the resort town of Rockaway Beach, New York:

In a family business, you always have to
sleep with one eye open. And nobody handles
the cash register but family. And then
you have to watch them, too.

Well into his lucrative speaking and broadcasting career,
McGuire was asked if he had enough money:

I have so much now I don't even count it. I weigh it.

◎

Yet, even after he became wealthy, McGuire would often try to save
a few bucks by asking a waitress or a store clerk:

Do you honor the clergy discount?

*On Rick Majerus, University of Utah coach and
an assistant at Marquette under McGuire, and the chances
that Majerus would play when, as a student,
he tried out for the Marquette team:*

I'd put the mascot in first.

On Hank Raymonds, McGuire's top assistant,
who succeeded McGuire as head coach:

Hank's a perfectionist. I've always said,
if he were married to Raquel Welch,
he'd expect her to cook.

To a priest in the Marquette president's office who was upset that McGuire had spurned an invitation in 1970 to the more prestigious NCAA tournament in favor of the National Invitation Tournament:

Father, I don't hear confession and you don't coach this team.

(McGuire recalled that twenty minutes after his statement, the priest called back and said, "You're right.")

○

After the university refused to release him from his contract when he wanted to take a $100,000 offer to coach the Milwaukee Bucks:

The priests at Marquette take a vow of poverty and they expect you to abide by it.

On the monks and other people who made an impression on McGuire when he coached at Belmont Abbey College in North Carolina:

They really opened a stained-glass window inside of me.

All right, let's show them we're
the number one team in the country
and beat the [bleep] out of them.
Queen of Victory, pray for us.

The Carnival Gates Close

McGuire Bids Farewell

5

During his final days, Al McGuire did things that were uncommon for him: he relived the glory days and he talked about death.

"He thought he'd take a pit stop into the oven" because he hadn't always done things right, recalled Ulice Payne Jr., one of the former Marquette players who reminisced with him in his hospice room. But McGuire figured he would end up in heaven, Payne said, because, all things considered, he had lived a pretty good life.

McGuire also worked to get his finances in order and made it a goal to live past certain tax deadlines so that he could get the best of the IRS.

McGuire crowed after living to see one more New Year's Day. "I'm ready now," Payne recalled him saying. "I beat Uncle Sam."

There's this big, gray elephant in the room and nobody wants to talk about it. But I know.

I'm movin' towards the dancin' lights.
Dancin' lights and a soft landing.

In those final days, Al McGuire the son told his father that he didn't have to struggle to get out of bed to hug each visitor. The father replied:

Son, I have to get up.
They have to remember me as being strong.

141

McGuire kept his humor to the end:

The doctors tell me that when I start coughing, it's pretty much over for me in three days. So I don't cough.

○

The University of Wisconsin was searching for a new basketball coach as McGuire lay dying. He joked to his son, Al:

Call the athletic director at the University of Wisconsin and tell him to take my name off the short list.

I'm dying with my eyes open.
I want to see everything.

It was nice to have had a chance
to soar with the eagles.

In 1996, saying he expected to live fifteen more years,
McGuire recalled how he shed tears during the final moments of
Marquette's national championship victory and said:

The next time I will cry is when I die.
My life has been that beautiful.

Right: McGuire takes a bow during a 1992 halftime ceremony
commemorating the 1977 NCAA championship team.

Chronology

Lexicon

Chronology

McGuire's Career

September 7, 1928: Born in New York.

1948–51: Plays basketball at St. John's University. Becomes team captain in 1951.

1951: Joins New York Knicks. After three seasons with Knicks (4.1 points per game on 38.4 percent shooting and 2.0 assists per game) is traded to Baltimore Bullets. NBA playing career ends when Bullets are disbanded after fourteen games.

1955: Becomes assistant coach at Dartmouth.

1957: Hired as head coach at Belmont Abbey. Posts 109–64 record in seven seasons.

April 11, 1964: Hired as head coach at Marquette at age thirty-five, succeeding Eddie Hickey.

1966–67: With star player George Thompson, leads Marquette to 21–9 record and gains first national acclaim with runner-up finish in the National Invitation Tournament. Warriors lose to Walt Frazier and Southern Illinois, 71–56, in title game at Madison Square Garden.

1967–68: Earns Marquette's first NCAA tournament bid since 1961 and finishes with 23–6 record.

1969–70: Angered that his 22–3 squad is placed outside the preferred Mideast Regional for the NCAA tournament, turns down the Warriors' invitation and takes team to NIT. Warriors beat St. John's for the title, finish season 26–3.

1971: Named college coach of the year by Associated Press, United Press International, the *Sporting News,* and the U.S. Basketball Writers Association.

1973–74: Advances to NCAA championship game, which Warriors lose, 76-64, to David Thompson and North Carolina State in Greensboro, North Carolina.

1974: Named coach of the year by the National Association of Basketball Coaches.

December 17, 1976: Stuns fans by announcing he will retire as coach after season to become vice chairman of Medalist Industries.

March 28, 1977: In last game as coach, leads Warriors to 67-59 victory over Dean Smith's North Carolina Tarheels for the NCAA championship.

October 10, 1977: Hired by NBC as a college basketball broadcaster.

1978: Lends name and support to Al's Run, a charitable 5-kilometer run that raises $2 million for Children's Hospital of Wisconsin through his final year of involvement in 1994.

1992: Hired by CBS as a college basketball analyst.

May 11, 1992: Inducted into Naismith Memorial Basketball Hall of Fame. Becomes part of the only set of brothers inducted into the hall when brother Dick is inducted in 1993.

March 5, 2000: Works final game as broadcaster, between Wisconsin and Indiana at the Kohl Center in Madison. Announces a few days later that he is suffering from some form of anemia.

July 27, 2000: Hospitalized for undisclosed illness, later determined to be leukemia. Transferred to hospice some days later.

January 26, 2001: Dies at age seventy-two.

Success at Marquette

McGuire's teams won 78.7 percent of their games in his thirteen years as coach of the Warriors (295–80).

He coached the team to eleven consecutive postseason bids.

His teams won at least twenty games in eleven of his thirteen years.

From 1969–77 only Marquette and UCLA finished in every Associated Press top fifteen final poll.

From 1967–73 Marquette had an 81-game home winning streak.

Only two other coaches have won the national title in their last college game—Larry Brown at Kansas in 1988 and John Wooden at UCLA in 1975.

His twenty-year record as a head coach is 404–144.

Lexicon

A McGuire Glossary

McGuire phrase	Translation
Go barefoot in the wet grass	Enjoy the moment
Congratulate the temporary	Live for the moment
Carnival gates are closed	Game's over
Salt and pepper coach	X's and O's coach
Cupcakes	Easy opponents
White knuckler	Close game
French pastry	A showy move
Cracked sidewalks	Bad part of town
Sand fights	Hard-fought games
Yellow ribbons and medals	Success in recruiting
Tailenders	Walk-ons or complementary players
Dunkirk	An extremely poor performance
Dance hall player	Short on talent, but long on effort
Memos and pipes	University administrators and professors
Two loaves of bread under their arms	Good jobs
Seashells and balloons	Victory and happiness
Curtains or tap city	Game's over
Aircraft carrier	Big center
Cloud piercer or ballerina in the sky	Player who jumps well
Thoroughbreds	Great players
Q-tips	Old people

Flush time	Halftime
Merry-go-round	The world of sports
Park Avenue	Anything first class
Tenth Avenue	Opposite of Park Avenue
Uptown	A post season invitation
Whistleblower	A coach who uses a lot of drills and likes his team to wear look-alike sport coats
Ten-percenter	Agent
Back room lawyer	Agent
Zebra	Referee

Credits

Pages ii, 13, 14, 23, 38, 41, 43, 44, 56, 69, 73, 76a, 76b, 76c, 76d, 76e, 76f, 76h, 76j, 76k, 76n, 79, 81, 82, 97, 103, 111, 119, 122, 123, 124,130, 131, 133, 141

Page 125

Pages 5, 6, 9, 11, 17, 21, 22, 27, 30, 31, 32, 34, 46, 52, 53, 55, 58, 62, 63, 75, 84, 87, 90, 92, 94, 95, 99, 100, 101, 102, 109, 112, 113, 135, 143, 147

Page 121

Pages 36, 76g, 76i

Pages 76l, 76m